Arizona Bark Scorpion

Threat: venomous sting

The Arizona Bark is thinner than its scorpion cousins and potentially the most lethal. Arizona State University produces a very effective anti-venin. Before the anti-venin was available, bark scorpions killed more people in Arizona than all the poisonous snakes combined. The Bark Scorpion stings with a series of quick jabs and then prefers to run rather than stand its ground. As their name suggests, they are often found on the underside of wood bark.

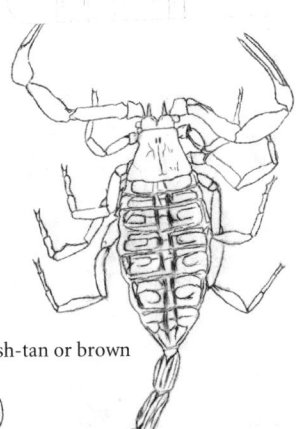

Color: light yellowish-tan or brown
Length: 2-3 inches

Giant Hairy Scorpion

Threat: venomous sting

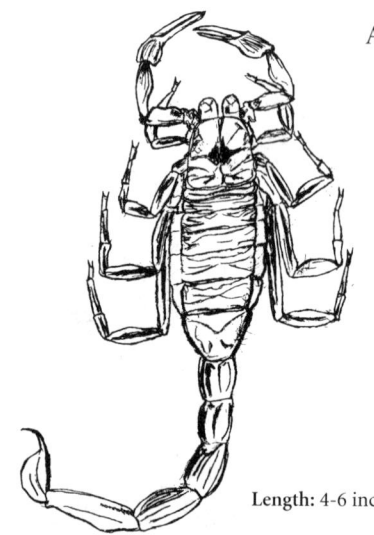

Arizona's largest scorpion is often found around suburban homes and garages as well as undeveloped areas. The Giant Hairy Scorpion frequently assumes a strong defensive posture when threatened, curling its body and tail high overhead and spreading its pincers. The stinging action is swift and well directed, but the sting is mild, usually causing only local pain and swelling.

Length: 4-6 inches

Introduction

Toxins are poisons produced in nature; this *Easy Field Guide*® is about those poisons. Venoms are toxins that are injected by a bite or sting. Nature's other toxins are absorbed through the blood stream, digestive tract, lungs or skin. They affect mucous membranes, tissues, or the circulatory system. Reactions can range from very mild irritation to severe discomfort and even death. Poisons affect individuals differently depending on their age, health and heredity.

Some potential sources of nature's poisons are not included in this guide. Your best approach is to treat all unknown plants and critters with respect. *Easy Field Guide*® *to Poisonous Plants and Critters of Arizona* may potentially help you identify and avoid some of nature's poisons. When exposure does occur, medical diagnosis and treatment are strongly recommended. Signs that an individual may have had contact with a toxin may include convulsions, diarrhea, numbness, rash, vomiting, and loss of appetite. Don't be shy about seeking help.

This *Easy Field Guide*® is part of a series that includes titles about common birds, cactus, fossils, insects, mammals, snakes, and trees of Arizona.

Striped-Tailed Scorpion

Threat: venomous sting

Like all of Arizona's scorpions, the Striped-Tailed has four pairs of jointed legs, an elliptical shaped body with a bulb-like poison gland and trademark stinger at the end of its tail. A stout tail with darkly-marked ridges running lengthwise along the underside differentiates Arizona's most common scorpion from its cousins. Usually under rocks or in a dark corner during the day, they venture from their shelters at night to forage and prey. The venom is generally mild but can be bothersome.

Length: 2 inches

Cone-Nose Bug

Threat: allergic reactions

Some folks call them Assassin Bugs and others call them Kissing Bugs. By any name, Cone-Nose Bugs are bloodsucking parasites. Although usually not painful, their bites can produce allergic reactions and are cause for concern. The head has four-segmented antennae, conspicuous eyes, and a three-segmented, straight beak that extends backward below the body. At rest, the wings are held flat over the back.

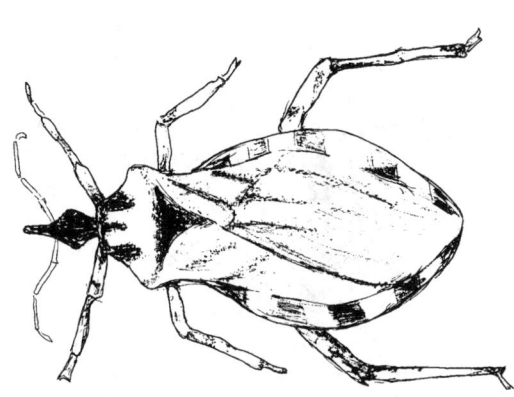

Color: brown to black on top
Length: ½ - ¾ inches

Mosquito

Threat: bite of the female

It is difficult to tell the many different species of mosquitos apart since their preferred feeding time is at dusk. The mosquito is a blood drinker and as such can carry disease from one animal or human to another as they feed. For example, in Arizona, mosquitoes have been the delivery system for West Nile Virus. Generally, they are just a nuisance that causes an itch and a small bump on your skin.

Puss Moth Caterpillar

Threat: allergic reaction

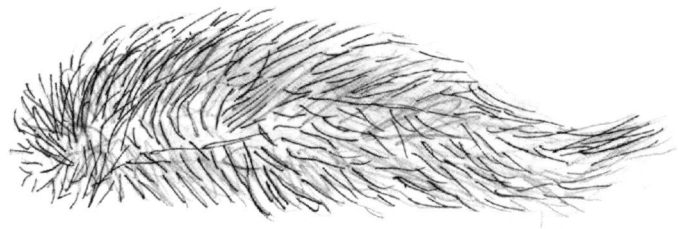

Several hairy caterpillar species have poison-gland cells. Brushing against their body can cause the release of toxins. Of these critters, the Puss Moth Caterpillar is considered by many to be Arizona's most poisonous. Hidden in its dense woolly coat are easily-broken hollow spines that deliver a dusting of toxin powerful enough to cause pain and allergic reaction comparable to a bee sting.

Puss caterpillars are completely covered with long, silken, brownish hairs about 1-inch long. The head and legs are not visible from above.

Giant Desert Centipede

Threat: venomous bite

The body of the Giant Desert Centipede is divided into 21 segments with one pair of yellow legs per segment; except the last pair of legs, which are orange and longer than the rest. Each of the legs is tipped with a sharp claw. Their jaws are connected to venom glands and are used to kill prey. Humans are not on their dinner menu but if you pick one up they are capable of injecting venom into your body. The bite is painful and usually causes swelling around the punctured area.

Legs: only 42, not 100

Length: 4-8 inches

Black Widow Spider

Threat: venomous bite

The Black Widow rarely causes death in a healthy victim, but by volume the venom is much more potent than that of the rattlesnake. The larger female carries more venom, consequently, her bite can be counted on to produce considerable discomfort. Most widows are black but some are brown or gray. The classic red marking can also be other bright colors and not necessarily in the notorious hourglass shape.

Color: shiny black
Length: 1½ inches

Brown Recluse Spider

Threat: venomous bite

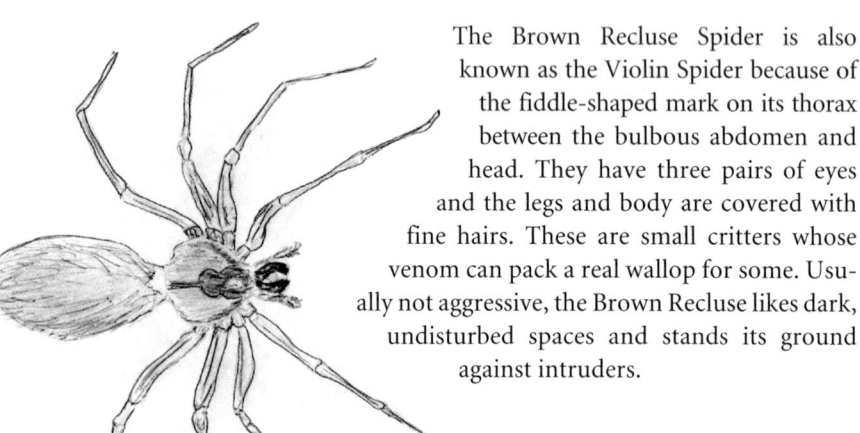

The Brown Recluse Spider is also known as the Violin Spider because of the fiddle-shaped mark on its thorax between the bulbous abdomen and head. They have three pairs of eyes and the legs and body are covered with fine hairs. These are small critters whose venom can pack a real wallop for some. Usually not aggressive, the Brown Recluse likes dark, undisturbed spaces and stands its ground against intruders.

Color: light tan to dark brown
Length: ¼-¾ inches

Tarantula

Threat: bite and for some the venom

Many consider the fearsome-appearing tarantula to be harmless. They have long hairy legs and a body covered with mouse-like fur. Some sport striking colors, others in Arizona are gray or dark brown. For most humans the bite is worse than the venom so take precaution to prevent infection from the bite wound. When the venom does have an effect, some numbness and itching may occur.

Color: varies
Leg span: up to 7 inches

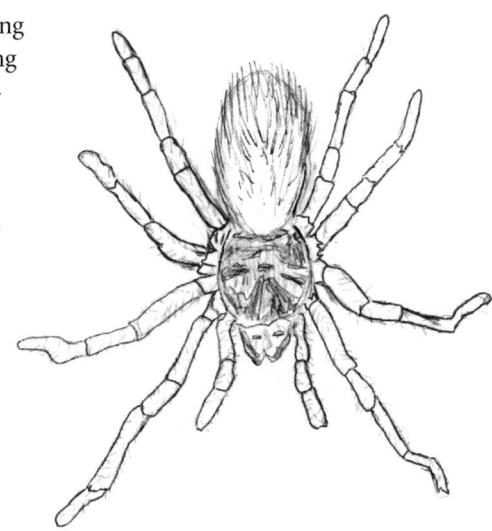

Ticks

Threat: spread of disease from a former host

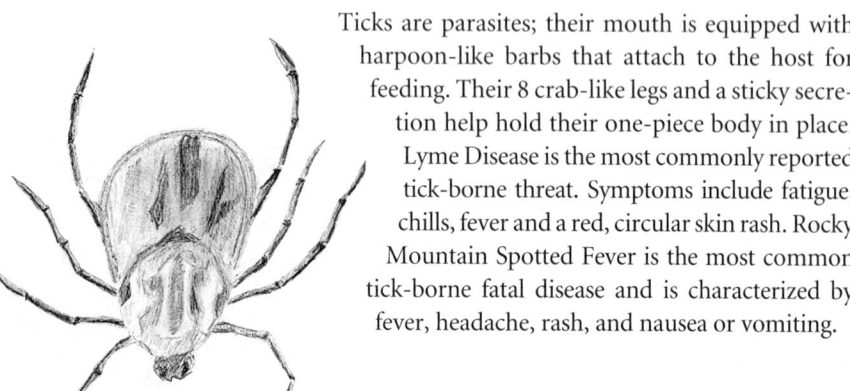

Ticks are parasites; their mouth is equipped with harpoon-like barbs that attach to the host for feeding. Their 8 crab-like legs and a sticky secretion help hold their one-piece body in place. Lyme Disease is the most commonly reported tick-borne threat. Symptoms include fatigue, chills, fever and a red, circular skin rash. Rocky Mountain Spotted Fever is the most common tick-borne fatal disease and is characterized by fever, headache, rash, and nausea or vomiting.

Color: dark brown to black
Size: a very small 3mm (= 0.118 inches)

Arizona Coral Snake

Threat: venomous bite

Length: 13-21 inches

Slender and relatively short, the Arizona Coral's venom is very potent. Because of the snake's small size, the bite does not pose as much danger to humans as that of the rattlesnake. However, as with any venomous reptile bite, medical treatment should start as soon as possible. The best way to identify the Arizona Coral is by the very blunt head that is black to behind the eyes, and its glossy red and black bands framed by either yellow or white bands.

Rattlesnakes

Threat: venomous bite

Arizona claims to have more species of rattlesnakes than any other state. The best way to recognize a rattlesnake is to see or hear the rattler. Almost all have a spade-shaped head. Their color patterns and body blotches range depending on the variety and habitat. The bands and patterns are usually quite distinct on the younger but can fade on older rattlers. The largest in both size and number is the Western Diamondback. The most venomous is the Mohave. The State Reptile is the Arizona Ridge-nosed Rattlesnake. Their venom breaks down blood and/or paralyzes nerves.

Length: 3-5 feet

Sidewinder

Threat: venomous bite

A member of the rattlesnake family, the Sidewinder is smaller than its cousins. Often found in arid flatlands, they are light in color with darker patches on the back. An upturned and pointed projection over the snake's eyes have earned the nickname Horned Rattler. The Sidewinder moves rapidly over desert surfaces using its unique *side-winding* locomotion. This viper's venom contains a moderate toxicity but still merits caution.

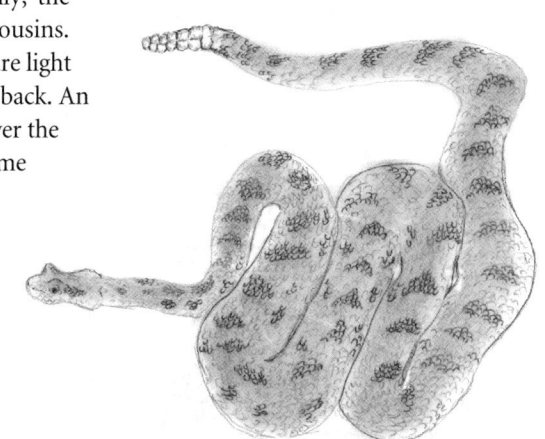

Length: 18-32 inches

Gila Monster

Threat: venomous bite

Gila monsters are bulky, slow-moving lizards that plod along on four short legs, dragging a blunt tail behind. Its studded skin has the appearance of black, pink, orange, and yellow beads, laid down in intricate patterns. Legend says the Gila Monster's breath can cause death but the real danger is the bite. The bite is normally not fatal to humans but the lumbering lizard can attack quickly and hold on tenaciously while small quantities of poison are injected through grooves in the teeth. To increase the effect, the Gila Monster chews its prey so as to put as much venom as possible into the bloodstream.

Length: 18-24 inches

Bees Wasps Ants

**Bees, Wasps and Ants are all distantly related.
Some bite, some sting, others do both.**

Bees

The Honeybee leaves his barbed-like-a-fish-hook stinger imbedded in your flesh. Other Arizona bees such as the Bumble and Carpenter Bee have sharper stingers and are capable of multiple attacks. Reactions to bee stings vary but the Carpenter Bee's venom is normally mild. The Africanized varieties usually carry less venom but are much more aggressive in defending their nest.

Wasps

Thinner and shinier than their thick-waisted bee cousins, wasps come in a variety of sizes and colors. Usually, the brighter the color the more painful the sting. Common to Arizona are Tarantula Hawk, Cicada Killer and Paper Wasps as well as the bright colored Yellowjackets and Hornets.

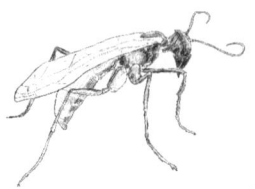

Ants

Many varieties of ants live in Arizona. Be especially alert for Harvester Ants whose heads are almost square. The Harvester's sting has been described as like "inserting a tiny red-hot needle into a pore and then having hot oil dripped on the surrounding skin." In addition to their potent sting, these ants can also bite ferociously.

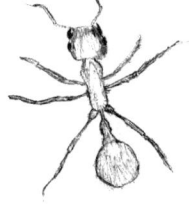

Fire Ant

Threat: venomous sting

Fire Ants are very aggressive and attack anything that disturbs them. After firmly grasping the skin with its jaws, the Fire Ant arches its back as it inserts its rear-end-mounted stinger into the flesh and injects venom from its poison sac. Then it pivots at the head and proceeds to inflict seven or eight more stings in a circular pattern. The venom injected produces a burning pain.

Colors: black and red

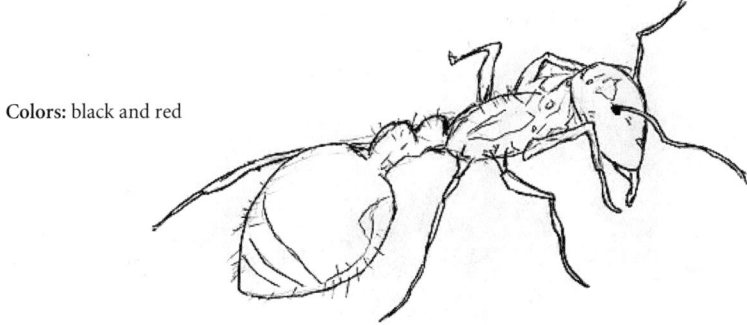

Velvet Ant

Threat: venomous sting

Several species of Velvet Ants live in Arizona. Actually wasps, the wingless females are the ones that look like hairy ants. The winged males are not a toxic threat since only the females have a stinger. Capable of stinging multiple times, they may warn of an impending attack with a squeaking, chirping sound or high pitched hum.

Size: ¼ - 1 inch
Colors: red, orange, yellow, silver, black and white

Rabies

Threat: bites

Rabies is a virus that lives in the saliva of infected mammals. It is usually more than a month after contact before noticeable symptoms occur. Rabies is almost always fatal if treatment is delayed until the symptoms appear. For this reason, it is essential to see a health care professional as soon as possible after exposure. In Arizona, the most common potential for exposure to rabies are bites from: bats (pictured), cattle, coyotes, foxes, mountain lions, raccoons and skunks. Any contact with a bat, dead or alive, should be considered a rabies exposure.

Bird of Paradise Shrubs

Toxic Part: pods and seeds

In Arizona, the name Mexican Bird of Paradise is routinely shared with its cousins the Red Bird of Paradise and the Desert Bird of Paradise. For all three, the 2-4 inch tan or yellowish seedpods are flat and the lima bean-shaped seeds are often toxic. The seeds of all scatter widely and can be a temptation to children and pets. Mexican and Desert Bird of Paradise flowers are yellow. The Red Bird of Paradise flowers can be orange as well as red.

Leaf Color: glossy dark or olive green
Height: up to 15 feet

Castor Bean

Toxic Part: seeds

Height: up to 40 feet

A large shrub, the Castor Bean usually has eight radiating, pointed leaflets with slightly serrated edges and prominent central veins. Most varieties are green, but some are reddish brown. The soft-spined fruits contain toxic seeds poisonous to people, animals and insects. The symptoms of human poisoning are abdominal pain, vomiting and diarrhea. Symptoms begin within a few hours of ingestion. Beware of necklaces made with Castor Bean seeds.

Mistletoe

Toxic Part: berries

Mistletoes are partial parasites that take water and nutrients from many different tree and shrub species. The variety depicted is both the kind reputed to evoke holiday kisses and produce a poisonous berry. Mistletoe often grows into large clumps accounting for its Navajo name "basket on high." No problem handling mistletoe stalks and leaves, but beware of the white berries; they are toxic, can cause cardiovascular collapse and can be fatal.

Mushrooms

Toxic Part: all

Sometimes referred to as toadstools, mushrooms are fleshy fungi that have a dome-shaped cap. However, not all mushrooms have stems. There are no simple tests to distinguish between edible and poisonous varieties. The only safe approach is to assume all wild mushrooms are poisonous since even small amounts are often very toxic.

Oleander

Toxic Part: all

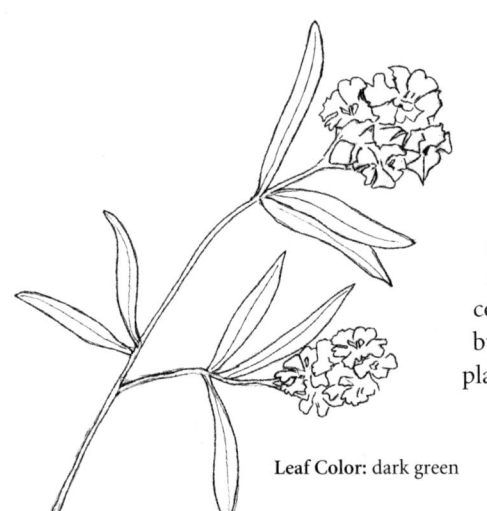

Leaf Color: dark green

Oleander shrubs have been used extensively in Arizona landscapes because they are evergreen and drought tolerant. Oleanders come in several different varieties ranging in height from 3 to 20 or more feet. The thick lance-like leaves can grow to lengths of more than 10 inches. The funnel-shaped flowers come in a range of colors and grow in clusters. Smoke from burning plant material can be as toxic as the plant material itself.

Poison Ivy

Toxic Part: urushiol

Poison Ivy is a woody vine that produces an oily substance called urushiol. Skin contact causes most people to develop a burning, itching skin rash that, once established, can spread rapidly. If you think you have come in contact, assume you're allergic. Wash yourself and everything that came in contact as soon as possible. It can take a day or two for the rash and blisters to manifest.

Leaf: green
Berries: white

Sago Palm

Toxic Part: all

Height: can reach 20 feet

Leaf Color: deep semi-glossy

The Sago Palm is a favorite container and landscape plant in Arizona. The ingestion of just one or two seeds can result in serious effects. The leaves have a rigid midrib with glossy leaflets. Those of the mature plant can be 18-45 inches long. The thick shaggy trunk is typically 8 inches in diameter. 50-100 year old specimens can grow as high as 20 feet.

Southwestern Thorn-Apple

Toxic Part: all

The large trumpet-shaped flowers of the Southwestern Thorn-Apple can be up to 6 inches long. They open late in the day and stay open till mid-morning. The spiny seed capsules are the most toxic part. Symptoms of contact include delirium, convulsions and coma. The Southwestern Thorn-Apple's close cousins Jimson Weed and Sacred Datura all look very much alike and are also toxic.

Flower Color: usually white
Height: up to 5 feet

Wisteria

Toxic Part: seeds and pods

Also known as the Kidney Bean Tree, Wisteria has sweet-pea-like flowers that cascade from its climbing woody vines. The pea-like seed pods are 4-6 inches long and contain toxic seeds. Many children have been poisoned by this plant.

Flower Color: blue, pink, purple, violet or white

Yew

Toxic Part: foliage

Often planted as an ornamental shrub or hedge, the Yew is a woody perennial with flat ½-1 inch long evergreen leaves. The leaves are toxic. Although the berry-like seed cones are edible, the hard seeds inside are extremely toxic, so don't take a chance. The toxins in this plant can attack the nervous system causing cardiac or respiratory collapse. Death usually occurs without any warning symptoms.

Leaves: dark green
Berries: maroon

Checklist and Index

- Arizona Bark Scorpion—*Centruroides sculpturatus* 3
- Arizona Coral Snake—*Micruroides euryxanthus* 13
- Bees, Wasps, Ants—*Hymenoptera* 17-18
- Bird of Paradise Shrub—*Caesalpinia* 22
- Black Widow Spider—*Scolopendra heros* 9
- Brown Recluse Spider—*Loxosceles reclusa* 10
- Castor Bean—*Ricinus communis* 23
- Cone-Nose Bug—*Triatoma* 5
- Fire Ant—*Solenopis Invicta* 19
- Giant Desert Centipede—*Scolopendra heros* 8
- Giant Hairy Scorpion—*Hadrurus arizonensis* 4
- Gila Monster—*Heloderma suspectum* 16
- Mistletoe—*Santalales* 24
- Mosquito—*Diptera* 6
- Mushrooms—*Fungi* 25
- Oleander—*Nerium oleander* 26
- Poison Ivy—*Toxicodendron radicans* 27
- Puss Moth Caterpillar—*Cerura vinula* 7
- Rabies—*rabies virus* 21
- Rattlesnakes—*Crotalus* 14
- Sago Palm—*Cycas revoluta* 28
- Sidewinder—*Crotalus cerastes* 15
- Southwestern Thorn-Apple—*Datura* 29
- Striped-Tailed Scorpion—*Vaejovis spinigerus* 2
- Tarantula—*Aphonopelma* 11
- Tick—*Acari* 12
- Velvet Ant—*Dasymutilla occidentalis* 20
- Wisteria—*Wisteria* 30
- Yew—*Taxus* 31